SNAKES AND OTHER REPTILES

by George S. Fichter

Illustrated by Sy Barlowe, James Gordon Irving, and others • Cover by Norman Adams

GOLDEN PRESS  NEW YORK

EDITORIAL ADVISORS

JOSETTE FRANK, *Director for Children's Books,
Child Study Association of America*
DR. LELAND B. JACOBS, *Professor of Education,
Teachers College, Columbia University*

Second Printing, 1969

© *Copyright 1968, 1965, 1960, 1953 by
Western Publishing Company, Inc.
Printed in the U.S.A.*

CONTENTS

What Is a Reptile?	4
Living Giants	10
How Long Do They Live?	14
Scales, Shells, and Horny Hides	18
Where They Live	24
How They Move	33
What Reptiles Eat	41
Most Reptiles Hatch From Eggs	52
Enemies	60
Self-Protection	67

FABLES
Snake Rolling Like Hoop
Bird Hypnotized by Snake

What Is a Reptile?

REPTILES are probably the most misunderstood animals in the world. So many myths and legends are believed about these creatures that it is truly difficult for people to learn the facts.

Many people still believe that snakes are slimy. Others are convinced that a turtle with its head cut off never dies until sundown. Some people think that a snake can hypnotize its prey with its steady, unblinking stare. And many are equally certain that "glass snakes" (which are really lizards) can break their bodies into pieces and then later reassemble themselves.

Alligators! Snakes! Lizards! Their very names stir the imagination. Through all human history reptiles have played prominent parts in folklore and religion. Rarely, except for turtles, have these roles been of the sort to make people think kindly of them. The story about the serpent in the Garden of Eden is an example. For this reason alone, to a great many people all snakes are treacherous, vile creatures.

Reptiles occupy the middle position in the five great groups of backboned animals. They are more advanced than fishes and amphibians, but they are lower in the scale of animal life than birds and mammals.

Reptiles do not have moist, slippery skins as do many amphibians. Instead, they are covered with dry scales or horny plates. They breathe air by means of lungs, and they either lay eggs or give birth to their young by keeping the eggs inside their bodies

FACTS

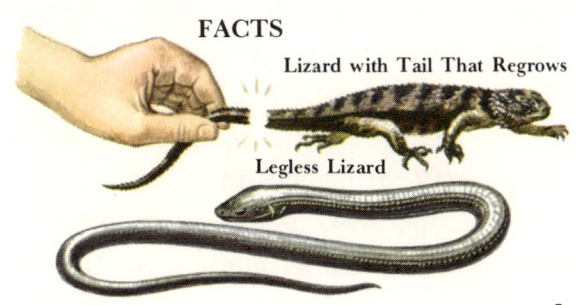

Lizard with Tail That Regrows

Legless Lizard

until they hatch. Young reptiles resemble the adults in appearance and habits. There is no bodily change—from egg to larva to adult—as in frogs and toads.

Yet reptiles, like amphibians and fishes, are cold-blooded animals. Unlike birds and mammals, which are warm-blooded, the body temperature of reptiles varies with their surroundings. This limits the places where reptiles can live and also the seasons and times of day when they can be active.

Reptiles living in temperate climates are generally active when the temperature is 70 degrees Fahrenheit or higher. Those that live in the tropics or in the hot deserts may require a higher temperature before they overcome their sluggishness. Horned toads, for example, are not very active at temperatures below 70 degrees. Many tropical reptiles prefer temperatures of 90 degrees or more. But reptiles die quickly from overheating if the temperature rises much above 110 degrees. When a reptile is in the hot sun, or after it has been moving rapidly, its body temperature may be actually higher than a bird's or a mammal's. Reptiles have no sweat glands or other cooling mechanisms in their skins. Even those that live in the desert do not expose themselves to the intense heat of the sun. During the day they hide in burrows, beneath rocks, or under plants. They come out in the cooler hours of early morning and late evening. Many are active only at night.

As the temperature drops below 70 degrees, reptiles become less and less active.

Snakes may hibernate in rock crevices, log piles, or burrows, and many share a den.

At 50 degrees, most of them no longer move about. Those living where winters are cold seek places to hibernate. Turtles may travel to springs where the temperature of the water stays about the same summer and winter. Many turtles bury themselves in the sand or mud when cold weather comes. Snakes and lizards hide in crevices, in burrows, or beneath rocks or logs. Sometimes many snakes use the same winter den.

Tuataras, or *Sphenodons,* are the most primitive of present-day reptiles. Found only in New Zealand, these sluggish, lizardlike creatures are of interest largely because this single species is the sole survivor of an ancient order of reptiles that was in existence before the days of the dinosaurs.

Studying tuataras helps scientists to better understand ancient reptiles.

Turtles hibernate in pockets in the sand during cold weather.

Turtles are also descended from an ancient order of reptiles that first appeared on the earth long before the Age of Dinosaurs. And present-day turtles look very much like those that lived 150 million years ago.

There are approximately 4,500 species of reptiles living today. This is only a fraction of the vast hordes of reptiles, large and small, that lived in ancient days.

In addition to the order to which the tuataras belong, there are three other orders still in existence: the order containing the crocodiles, gavials, and alligators, with about 25 species; the turtles and tortoises, with approximately 225 species; and the lizards and snakes, each with more than 2,000 species.

Enormous flippers and seven thick ridges on its back distinguish the leatherback turtle.

Living Giants

THE days of the great dinosaurs are long past, but among our modern-day reptiles, there are many giants, too.

Several kinds of huge sea turtles inhabit warm ocean waters throughout the world. Largest of these is the leatherback. A leatherback caught off the coast of Canada weighed 1,500 pounds and had a flipper spread of eight feet. It is believed that some of these big turtles may weigh as much as a ton.

Records also show that green turtles sometimes exceed 800 pounds in weight, although any that weigh more than 400 pounds are considered large. Interestingly, a green turtle that weighs less than 125 pounds is called a "chicken" by commercial turtle fishermen.

Largest of the fresh-water turtles is the alligator snapper found in southern United States. It is known to reach a weight of about 200 pounds and may grow even larger.

On land there are bulky, elephant-footed tortoises. Several kinds found in Africa and Asia weigh about 100 pounds, but the largest tortoises live on the volcanic Galapagos Islands about 600 miles off the west coast of South America. One of these giants may weigh 550 pounds or more.

Snakes attain their greatest size in the tropics. Regal pythons of Asia were long believed to be the largest snakes. A specimen measuring 32 feet in length was recorded. However, equally reliable reports recently have come from the jungles of South America, recording anacondas with lengths of 37 and 38 feet. Anacondas are much heavier than the slimmer pythons. A 20-foot anaconda, for example, may weigh nearly 250 pounds, perhaps 100 pounds more than a python of the same length.

Other giant snakes include the poisonous bushmasters of Central America. They may exceed 12 feet in length, while the deadly king cobras of Asia may be more than 18 feet long. In the United States, the eastern diamondback rattlesnake occasionally approaches eight feet in length and may be bigger around than a man's arm.

Largest of the lizards is the Komodo dragon, found only on the East Indian islands of Komodo, Rintja, Padar, and West Flores.

Komodo dragons are the largest lizards. They are immensely strong and fierce, and may grow up to 10 feet in length.

This giant lizard reaches a length of 10 feet and may weigh 200 pounds or more. The Komodo dragon is a monitor lizard. There are a number of kinds of monitors found in Africa and Asia, and several species are five or six feet in length. The common iguana is equally large, but more than four feet of its length is its long, whiplike tail. The longest lizard in the United States is the glass snake, which is sometimes more than three feet long. Bulkiest are the Gila monster and the chuckwalla. Both measure about two feet in length and have heavy bodies.

Still the most fearsome of all reptiles in appearance, speed, and ferocity are those near-relatives of the ancient dinosaurs—the alligators, crocodiles, and gavials. Most members of this ancient group are six feet long or longer. The smallest is the dwarf crocodile of Africa, and it averages three feet in length.

Crocodiles are known to reach a length of 23 feet. Gavials exceed 20 feet, and the American alligator, while seldom more than 12 feet long now, was reported to reach a length of more than 19 feet in years gone by.

Galapagos Tortoise

Tortoises and men are the longest-lived animals.

How Long Do They Live?

TORTOISES and man live longer than any other animals. There are records to indicate that individuals of both species have passed the age of 150. And one tortoise, which is known to have lived in captivity for the almost unbelievable period of 152 years, may have been 25 or even 50 years old at the time of its capture!

Often the ages of reptiles are exaggerated. It used to be thought, for example, that any large alligator or crocodile was certainly several hundred years old. Now it is known that these reptiles rarely pass the age of 50. The record for an American alligator in captivity is 56 years.

Common box turtles, too, may often reach the age of 50, and records indicate that some may have lived for more than a century.

People who find box turtles frequently carve their name and the date into the turtles' shells before turning them loose. Sometimes the dates are hard to read when the turtles are found again, and if there is a question, storytellers pick the date that makes the best story. Or perhaps a prankster will carve in the name of some famous person of a century or more ago. You can find such names as George Washington, Daniel Boone, or Thomas Jefferson inscribed in turtle shells. You can also find turtles bearing dates that make them older than the discovery of America! These make interesting newspaper stories.

The most reliable records on ages of reptiles come from zoos and wildlife parks, and from pet owners who have accurately recorded their pets' dates of capture. One tortoise in an eastern zoo is now over 50 years old. It was captured by Theodore Roosevelt. A black-lipped cobra lived for more than 29 years in a zoo, while an anaconda lived for 28 years in a zoo, and a rainbow boa lived for 27 years. A number of snakes have lived longer than 20 years in captivity, and a slow-worm, a legless lizard of Europe, lived for 32 years.

Much of the misunderstanding about how long reptiles live was based on the belief that they grow very slowly. Only recently have we learned how rapidly they do grow. Green turtles can grow shells four feet long in as short a time as 10 years. They do not

Some box turtles may have lived more than a century although most live about 50 years.

become much larger after reaching this size, although they may live for many more years. Galapagos tortoises have reached a weight of 400 pounds in only 15 years. Alligators and crocodiles grow about 12 inches a year. An American alligator, for example, may be about five feet long and weigh 50 pounds at five years. When it is 10 years old, it may be nearly 10 feet long and weigh about 250 pounds. From this point on, it grows more slowly.

Now and then, just as is true of human beings, a few individuals among reptiles manage to stretch their years well past the average.

Crocodiles and alligators may live
50 years, perhaps even longer.

Scales, Shells, and Horny Hides

ONE of the big differences between reptiles and amphibians is their outer coverings. A typical amphibian's skin is moist and soft. This makes it necessary for amphibians to live in water or in moist surroundings. But reptiles have dry skins. They can live in a greater variety of land situations. Many kinds live in deserts, among rocks, or in trees.

Snakes and lizards are covered with scales over which there is a thinner, transparent layer of skin. Several times each year this skin is shed, depending on how much the snake or lizard has grown. A well-fed snake, for example, may shed its skin five or six times in a season.

Just before a snake sheds its skin, the transparent caps over its eyes become milky. For a week or more the snake is almost blind. During this time the skin loosens over its body, and its colors become dull.

A snake begins to shed by rubbing its nose against some sharp object to loosen its skin.

Lizard Skin

Frog Skin

Reptiles have dry skins; amphibians have moist ones.

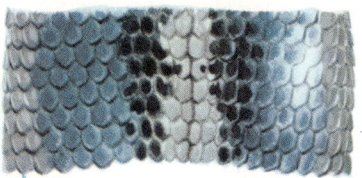
Belly Scales—LIZARDS

Belly Scales—SNAKES

Cross Section of Rattle

Button

Young

Older

Adult

Old Adult

A lizard has eyelids and ear openings.

Copperhead Shedding

A snake may shed its skin several times a year.

Then it crawls out, turning its skin inside-out. The rattlesnake's rattle at the end of its tail consists of unshed layers of horny skin held together loosely in "buttons." These make a noise when the snake's tail is vibrated in nervous excitement.

Some lizards crawl out of their old, loose skins; others shed the skin in patches. The scales covering a lizard's belly are much like those on its back. Snakes, however, have single, wide scales, or scutes, on their bellies. This is one way of distinguishing a "legless" lizard from a snake. Typically, of course, a lizard has four legs. It also has eyelids and external ear openings, while a snake does not. Snakes have forked tongues, but most lizards do not.

Most unusual are the scales of the Gila monster. They do not overlap, as do the scales

The Gila Monster has beadlike scales.

on most lizards and snakes, and they are rounded so that they look like beads. Hence, another common name for the Gila monster is "beaded lizard."

Crocodiles and alligators are covered with a thick, horny skin which forms heavy ridged scales over their backs and tails. They do not shed their skins, but the old, worn portions are replaced by new growth from underneath. The skin on their bellies is processed to make durable leather products, such as belts, shoes, and handbags. Many thousands of alligators and crocodiles are slaughtered by hide hunters every year. The skins of some snakes and lizards are also tanned to make leather.

Turtles have the most unusual skeletons of any of the backboned animals. Their bodies are tucked between two bony shells. The upper, often domelike half of the shell is called the carapace. The flat lower half is called the plastron.

The common box turtle has such a high-arched shell that it can draw its head and legs completely inside. Its plastron is hinged in the middle so that the shell can be closed

The carapace and plastron form the shell.

tightly. In contrast, soft-shelled turtles have flexible shells covered with a soft, leathery skin. Giant marine leatherbacks have a similar leathery "shell" thickened to form seven heavy ridges.

Covering the bony portions of the typical turtle's shell are horny plates, or scutes. In

Soft, leathery skin covers the bony parts of the soft-shelled turtle.

Tortoise shell comes from the carapace of the hawksbill turtle.

Bony plates lie under the horny scales of the crocodile.

some turtles these are shed periodically. It is the coloring and sculpturing of these scutes that give a turtle its distinctive appearance.

The shields of the sea-dwelling hawksbill turtles were once an important item of commerce. Carefully peeled from the shell and then polished, they became the "tortoise shell" used in making combs and pins. Tortoise shell has been largely replaced by plastics.

Turtle shells also serve as rattles and decorative ornaments in ceremonial dances of some primitive peoples. And there was an ancient belief that the weight of the world was supported on the sturdy shell of a gargantuan turtle.

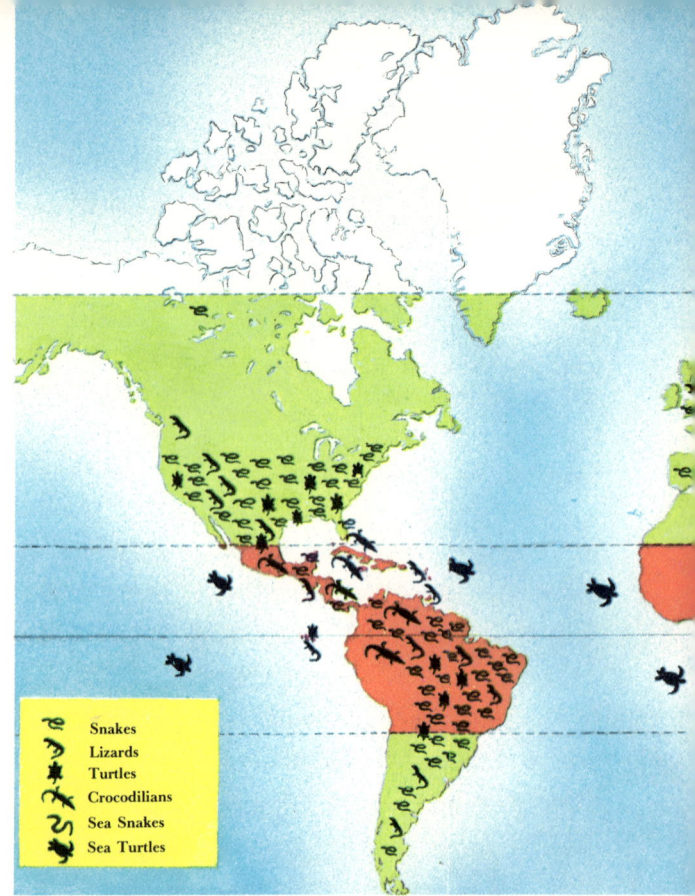

Where They Live

REPTILES inhabit every continent of the world except Antarctica. But they are most abundant, both in numbers and in kinds, in tropical regions.

The map above shows where the different kinds of reptiles live throughout the world. The greatest proportion of reptiles inhabit the warmer regions.

Surprisingly, since they are cold-blooded creatures, two species do live within the Arctic Circle. These are the common viper and the green lizard found in the Scandinavian countries of Europe. Both bear their young alive, for the climate in which they live is too cold for the development of eggs laid on land.

Most reptiles live where the temperature never drops below freezing. Thus, they are more numerous closer to the equator. In the United States, for example, there are more reptiles in Florida than in Maine and more in Arizona than in Montana. Snakes and turtles live farther north than do lizards, which are most abundant in the Southwest. Alligators are found only in the South, and crocodiles are confined to the tip of Florida.

Some reptiles long ago returned to the water to live. Even these reptiles, however, still breathe air. Turtles come out on land to lay their eggs, but most water snakes give birth to their young in the water, carrying the eggs inside their bodies until they hatch.

In the Pacific Ocean off the continent of Asia, there are about 50 kinds of sea snakes. They developed from cobralike snakes, and all of them are deadly poisonous. Fortunately, they are gentle. Their tails and often their entire bodies are flattened from side to side for swimming. Their lungs are large, so they can take in enough air to last them as long as eight hours without coming to the surface. Their nostrils can be closed off when they submerge.

Sea turtles are widely distributed in warm seas throughout the world. Their legs have become flippers used for swimming. Some kinds of sea turtles range over hundreds of miles of open ocean, often straying into cold latitudes following the ocean currents. A green turtle's home may be a hole in the coral, or it may be a bare, rocky spot in a great pasture of seaweeds. Here the turtle spends its nights sleeping, rising several times to take in new supplies of air. After the turtles have gone to bed at night, turtle fisher-

Sea turtles inhabit the warm waters of the oceans throughout the world. Green turtles are the species most used commercially.

men set their nets over the holes to catch the turtles when they come up for air.

The green turtles of the Caribbean are believed to have a homing instinct. Several times, at least, green turtles caught and branded off the coast of Nicaragua have escaped captivity in Key West, Florida, and were recaptured months later in their old haunts, some 800 miles south of Key West. Since the island of Cuba lies between the two places, the turtles had to navigate around it to get home.

On the Galapagos Islands, there are some enormous lizards that spend part of their time in the sea. These ferocious-looking iguanas are not dangerous. They actually refuse to bite. Diving from the rocks into the sea, they feed on sea lettuce and other marine plants.

Crocodiles and the sharp-snouted gavials also live in salt or brackish waters on or near the coast.

Many kinds of turtles and snakes live in fresh water. Alligators, too, prefer fresh water and spend a good part of their time submerged—or nearly so. Their nostrils are bulbs

Crocodiles hunt their prey at the water's edge.

on top of their snouts, and their eyes also stick up like knobs above the level of their heads. So an alligator can lie in the water with only its nostrils and eyes sticking out. When it submerges, valves close its nostrils. It also has flaps covering the openings to its ears, and a valve in its throat shuts off its windpipe so that it can open its mouth underwater to grab food without taking water into its lungs.

Most reptiles, however, live on land. They occupy every sort of habitat available above ground. Some even burrow into the soil. Worm lizards and worm snakes, for example, are blind and spend their lives tunneling in loose soil in search of worms and insects.

A great many kinds of reptiles live in the deserts. As a rule, these reptiles are active at night, for they cannot survive the hot sun. Often their eyes are larger than average so that they can see even at night or in the dim light of dusk and dawn. During the day they hide in burrows or under rocks or plants.

Some kinds of desert snakes and lizards have broad, shovel-shaped snouts for digging into the sand. They can literally "swim" into the sand and out of sight. Others have flattened toes so that their feet act like snowshoes. They can run rapidly over the sand without sinking in. Fringe-toed lizards are good examples. Sidewinder rattlesnakes loop their bodies sideways, providing a broad, flat surface as they crawl, so that they do not push into the sand.

Many of the burrowers have special scales that fold over their eyes and nostrils to keep the sand out. Desert, or gopher, tortoises dig

Fringe on the feet of sand lizards aids them in running over loose, soft sand.

Zebra-tailed Sand Lizard

Fringe-footed Sand Lizard

long underground burrows and return to them after feeding all night on grass and other plants.

In the wet tropics, where a large percentage of animals are adapted to living in the trees, some lizards scamper about in the vines and branches as agilely as squirrels. Chameleons have opposing toes on their feet, and grasping tails, which they use to hold onto their perches. Many snakes of the tropics are slim. They travel through branches feeding on birds and eggs.

Reptiles, with few exceptions, are not conspicuous, nor are they bold. Often a careful search of an area by an expert reveals many reptiles that an average person does not see. Once, a naturalist on his first trip to Africa remarked about the scarcity of reptiles. He had seen none. His guide promptly staked off an area of about an acre, and in combing that plot of ground, they discovered more than a hundred different specimens hidden in the undergrowth.

The long-nosed tree snake is well-hidden among the green vines of the tropic forests.

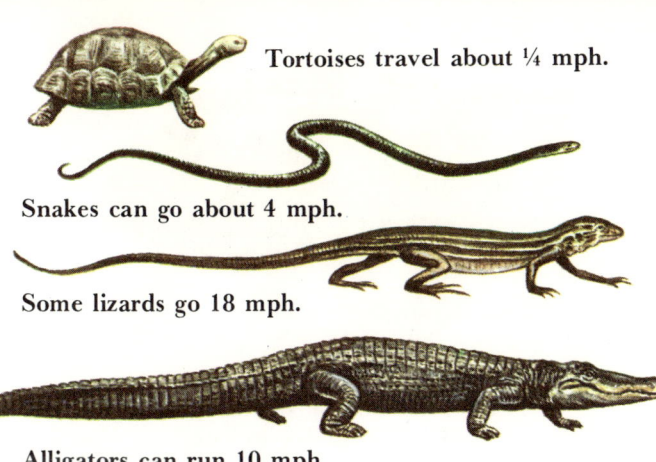

Tortoises travel about ¼ mph.

Snakes can go about 4 mph.

Some lizards go 18 mph.

Alligators can run 10 mph.

Sea turtles can swim 20 mph or faster.

How They Move

EVERY spring certain Florida communities stage one of their most interesting events of the year: a tortoise race. Tortoise is pitted against tortoise rather than against a hare, as in the hare and tortoise race of the famous fable.

Before the race begins, the tortoises are placed in the center of a circle that is 30 feet or more in diameter. At the signal of the starting gun, the crowd cheers wildly for the racers to be off.

The loggerhead turtle's flippers are adapted for swimming but this turtle must drag itself along on land.

Some of the tortoises never budge from their tracks. Others—and tortoises are notoriously never in a hurry to go anywhere—begin plodding toward the outer edge of the circle. Now and then one that looks like a sure winner gets tired before it comes to the finish line and stops for a prolonged rest. Or another may be about to step across the line when it turns back toward the center again. But eventually some tortoise does unwittingly stumble over the finish line.

It is an exciting and sometimes uproarious affair for the human spectators. But the tortoises take the whole event in stride—*their* stride, naturally. At top speed this moves them along at about a quarter of a mile per hour.

An opposite extreme from these trudgers are the sea turtles, which are surprisingly swift and graceful. Loggerhead turtles have been clocked doing 30 feet per second (about 20 miles per hour), but biologists say that loggerheads are slow in comparison to the speedy leatherbacks which live in deeper water farther out at sea.

Equally fast, even though much smaller, are some of the fast-running lizards of the

The collared lizard has a very long tail and sometimes runs on its hind legs.

desert. Collared lizards, for example, stand up on their hind legs and sprint off with astonishing speed. Racerunners can run 18 miles per hour.

Big monitor lizards sometimes dive into the water when frightened. Few lizards are good swimmers, however. Geckos hold fast to limbs with the tiny hooks on the pads of their toes. They can even run upside down across a ceiling. And one of the Asiatic geckos is an excellent glider. Like the flying squirrel, it has a membranous "wing" between its fore and hind legs. It jumps from one tree and glides to the next.

Another Asiatic lizard is known as the "flying dragon." Its ribs are extra long, and they can be lifted so that loose folds of skin along the sides of its body are spread tightly over them. This makes the "wings" which the lizard uses in gliding. Often bright warning colors show when the wings are spread.

One of the most unusual sights is a Central American basilisk streaking away in fright. This lizard has a crest on its head and also has a slim whiplike tail. The basilisk runs on its hind legs, often so rapidly that

The basilisk's long tail balances it when it runs on its hind legs.

both hind feet are off the ground at the same time. Oddly, if it comes to a pool or a stream, it can run right across the surface without sinking in.

Snakes probably do not move nearly as fast as most people think they do. Some of the racers have been clocked at three and a half miles per hour, but anyone would guess that they were going much faster.

When a snake is not in a hurry, it moves forward in a straight line. It presses its body tightly against the ground to get traction. It does not use its ribs as legs but pulls itself along with the edges of its plates, caterpillar-fashion. Moving in this fashion, a snake seems to flow along the surface.

But when a snake is in a hurry, it wiggles its body rapidly so that it makes a series of "s" shapes. Each loop pushes against any bump or irregularity it contacts on the surface so that the snake literally swims across the ground. It follows that snakes are naturally good swimmers, for in swimming they use this same type of wiggling movement.

Snakes have several hundred ribs. However, snakes appear to move by using their scales, which catch in irregularities of the surface of the ground.

Boas and pythons, incidentally, have tiny claws on the undersurface of their bodies near their tails. This is evidence of the close relationship of snakes to lizards.

In Asia there are several snakes that can glide from tree to tree. These "flying snakes" have elongated ribs, like those of the flying dragon. When their ribs are extended, their bodies become flattened; at the same time they expel the air from their lungs so that their bodies are almost as thin as a leaf when they take to the air. As soon as they land, they fold their ribs back in place again, and they take in a new supply of air. They look like normal round-bodied snakes once more.

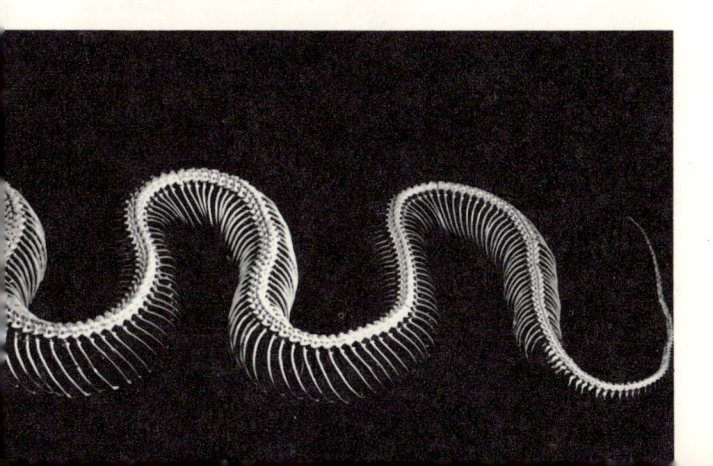

Alligators and crocodiles, while they appear to be lumbering, clumsy beasts, can be astonishingly fast. Angered, they can attack with lightning speed. Frightened, they can run away so fast that a man cannot overtake them. When an alligator or a crocodile is moving rapidly on land, it stands high on its legs and actually runs on its toes. In the water, it folds its legs close to its body and swims by wiggling its whole body. Most of the propelling force comes from its tail.

The whipsnake, one of the fastest snakes, can only go about 3½ miles per hour.

Hognosed snakes prey on cold-blooded creatures such as frogs and toads.

What Reptiles Eat

MOST reptiles eat other animals. Some eat only warm-blooded animals; others, only cold-blooded animals. Fewer kinds are strictly vegetarian. If their favorite food is not available, most reptiles will quickly select a substitute. Only a few are highly specialized in their food habits.

Box turtles, for example, will eat insects, worms, and other small animals found crawling about on the forest floor. But they also like fruits and berries. Now and then someone finds a box turtle that has discovered a berry patch and stayed there until it has become so fat that it can no longer get its head and legs into its shell.

Giant tortoises are vegetarians. Those in captivity can be coaxed to plod along taking children for rides on their backs. With a banana or an apple tied to a string, a skilled lad at the helm can steer one of these "living tanks" just about anywhere he wants to go—if he is in no hurry about getting there.

A few turtles have developed unusual eating habits or methods of getting their food.

A spotted turtle can eat only when its head is underwater.

Spotted turtles that inhabit fresh-water ponds in eastern United States eat a variety of insects, snails, and other animal life found in the water and along its edge. But oddly, they can eat only when their heads are under the water.

Alligator snappers, which live in the swamps of southern United States, are lazy reptiles with big appetites. Covered with moss, leeches, mud, and debris, they are difficult to distinguish from the rocks or logs in their environment. When an alligator snapper is hungry, it opens its huge mouth and lures its dinner inside. The lining of its mouth is mottled in color and has fringes of skin that wave in the water and help to conceal its outline. On the front edge, acting as a lure, is its tongue—a finger-like projection which stands erect whenever the turtle's mouth is open. In a young turtle, this thin tip of its tongue is red and looks like a worm. In older turtles, it is white. It wiggles enticingly and attracts the attention of passing fish. But woe be it to any fish that decides this would make a good meal. For a fish that is duped into making a dash at the "worm" suddenly finds itself inside the turtle's mouth with the great jaws snapped tightly shut.

A South American turtle also has a strange way of catching fish. When it sees a likely meal approaching, this turtle quickly opens its mouth and expands its throat. Water rushes in to fill the gaping mouth and throat cavities, and the fish is literally sucked in.

Turtles, incidentally, do not have teeth. Most of them have sharp, cutting edges on their jaws, and these may also be saw-toothed so that they function as teeth to help tear the food into chunks.

Among snakes, a few species have specialized food habits. European grasshopper vipers subsist only on grasshoppers. In Mexico and Central America there are snakes that prefer snails and slugs. The queen snake found in fresh waters in the United States prefers crayfish, and one of the rear-fanged snakes of Java lives on crabs.

Egg-eating snakes of Africa have developed highly specialized equipment for eating eggs. In their throats there are razor-sharp projections from their vertebrae. As soon as

A snake's mouth and body can stretch over large eggs. In one African snake the egg is then slit by modified vertebrae in the snake's upper body.

an egg has been swallowed to this point, the snake constricts its throat and slices through the egg's shell. Then the shell is easily crushed by more tightening of the throat muscles, and its contents flow into the snake's stomach while the shell is regurgitated.

Snakes always swallow their food whole and are truly remarkable in being able to swallow animals with bodies larger in diameter than their own. They accomplish this feat by possessing an extra joint in their lower jaws that allows extra expansion, and also stretching them at the front where the two halves are joined by an elastic ligament. Then the food is worked in slowly as the snake moves first one side of its jaw forward, then the other. Its teeth curve back so that even if its prey is still alive and kicking it is not likely to get free.

If the prey is large, the snake may swallow it slowly, requiring several hours to finish its meal. Its skin stretches and its ribs, which are loosely connected to its backbone, lift over the food as it is engulfed. Anacondas and pythons are large enough to eat animals the size of a deer or a pig.

All snakes are carnivorous. They have strong digestive juices which soon dissolve the food, even such ordinarily indigestible substances as bones and shells. These strong juices, incidentally, make impossible the old folk story that the mother snake swallows her young when they are endangered by enemies. The young could not survive long in their mother's stomach.

Many snakes have diets that are beneficial to man. This is especially true of those that eat rodents. The pretty scarlet and gray milk snake in the United States does not milk cows, for example. It got its name from being seen frequently around cow barns, and people began to believe that it was there to steal milk. Actually, it eats mice.

Pilot black snakes, corn snakes, fox snakes, and racers are also rat and mouse eaters. They have an advantage over cats, too, for

Constrictors, such as the corn snake, kill their prey by squeezing it to death.

they can crawl into the rat or mouse den and rob the nest of its young. This eliminates the rodents before they can breed and become even more numerous.

These typical rodent eaters are nonpoisonous. Some of them kill their prey before swallowing it. This they do by coiling their bodies around the animal and squeezing it tightly. These snakes are called constrictors. They are able to determine exactly when their victim has died. Not until then do they release their coils. Others swallow their prey while it is still alive, generally holding it in place with loops of their bodies until they have swallowed it far enough so that it no longer struggles violently.

Poisonous snakes paralyze or kill their prey before they eat it. Pit vipers use their "pits," located between their nostrils and their eyes, to detect the body heat of an animal at night and can determine the striking range with great accuracy. Both snakes and lizards employ their tongues as tasters, smellers, and feelers in locating their food.

Oddly, there are some kinds of snakes that specialize in eating other snakes. Members of the cobra family are notorious snake eaters, and some of them will eat no other food. In the United States, king snakes and whipsnakes, while harmless themselves, will attack and devour rattlesnakes. King snakes are immune to the rattlesnake venom.

Lizards do not have doubly hinged jaws. Many of them are spider and insect eaters and have specialized tongues for capturing their prey. Most remarkable of these is the tongue of the chameleon, which is fully as long as the chameleon itself. At its tip there is a sticky bulb. As the chameleon begins to move in on an insect, its tongue shoots out faster than a human eye can follow—and also faster than an insect's, for the chameleon rarely misses its meal. The chameleon's pro-

Many lizards like the ground uta live on a diet of insects.

truding eyes, incidentally, can be moved independently. One may be looking in the branches overhead, while the other is scanning those underneath. But when the lizard strikes, both eyes focus directly on its target.

The giant Komodo dragons, of course, need proportionately larger prey. They capture and consume deer or pigs. Other monitor lizards, such as those living in Africa, prey on reptiles and rodents, while the large land iguanas of the Galapagos Islands are plant eaters. They like the flowers, leaves, and spines of cacti. Cacti flowers are also a favorite food of the chuckwallas and crested lizards. Gila monsters prey on fledgling birds and young mammals.

Alligators, gavials, and crocodiles, when full grown, feed largely on fish. The slim snouts of the gavials are especially suited for catching fish. But they also eat birds, mammals, or any other creature that is unwary enough to come within their reach. Occasionally an alligator will come out on land and stalk its prey. Sometimes they become bold enough to attack dogs or pigs.

An alligator or a crocodile cannot swal-

The slender snout of the gavial helps it to catch fast-swimming fish.

low large prey whole. Generally, it drowns its prey. It holds the animal firmly between its jaws and then lashes it back and forth violently. This tears the prey apart, and the alligator then consumes the pieces.

Reptiles do not consume large quantities of food, for they do not have to maintain a high body temperature, as do birds and mammals. During warm weather, and if food is available, snakes may eat regularly and shed often. In cool weather, they may eat nothing.

Baby turtles have an egg tooth with which they cut themselves out of their shells.

Most Reptiles Hatch From Eggs

ONE of the great advances reptiles made over their amphibian ancestors was the ability to lay eggs which could develop on land. This made it possible for them to live in deserts, fields, and forests without having to return to the water to live at any stage of their lives. In fact, the opposite became necessary for aquatic reptiles. Those that lay eggs, such as the turtles, must come out on land to do so.

Reptile eggs look a lot like bird eggs. Some are almost perfectly round, like ping-pong balls; others are oblong. But instead of being covered by a fragile lime shell, reptile eggs have leathery, soft shells which are porous. The embryos inside breathe through the shell membrane.

Most reptiles lay their eggs in loose soil or in decaying vegetation and leave them there to be incubated by the heat of the sun. Some lay only a few eggs. House geckos, for example, lay only one. Others, such as the sea turtle, lay several hundred eggs. As a rule, reptiles place their eggs in some sort of a nest and give them no further attention. Generally the eggs hatch within a few weeks, but those of the primitive New Zealand tuatara incubate for more than a year before the young emerge. Before it hatches, an incubating reptile egg actually increases in size, often becoming a third or more larger than it was at the time it was laid.

Young reptiles cut their way out of the tough egg membrane by means of an "egg tooth" that develops at the end of their snouts. Within a day or two this temporary tooth drops off, having served this one important function.

Pythons are exceptions among reptiles in that they incubate their eggs themselves. The female coils around them, and her own body temperature will increase several degrees during the incubation period. Common

Some species of skinks stay with their eggs until they hatch.

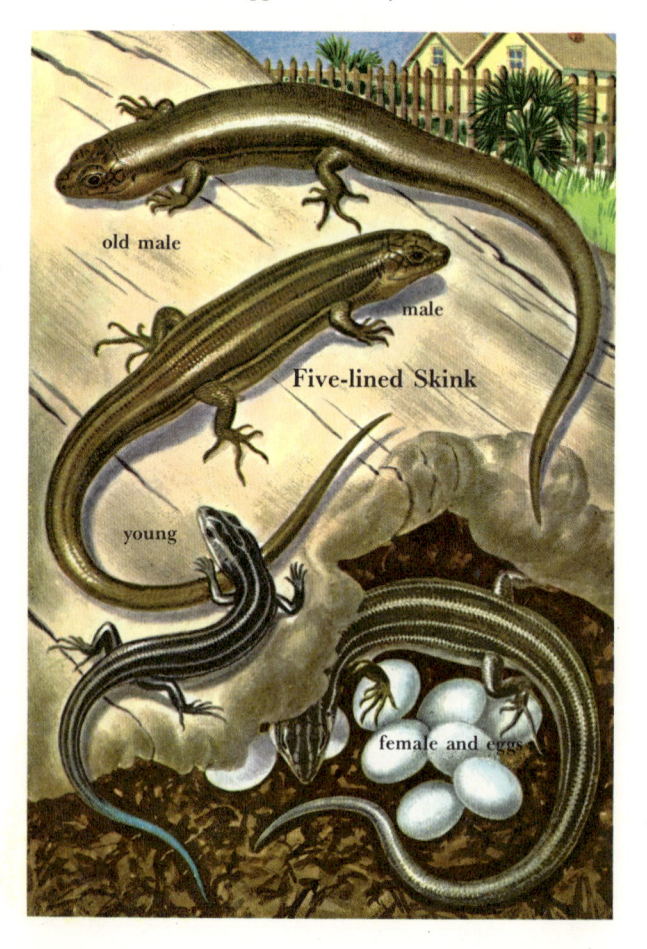

skinks, cobras, and bushmasters are among the few other reptiles which stay with their eggs until they hatch.

Alligators give their nests and eggs exceptional attention. Before she lays her eggs, the female laboriously gathers plants and sticks, and piles them into a mound several feet high. Thus, when her eggs are laid, they will be well above the normal high-water mark in the swamps where the alligator lives.

In the scooped-out center of this nest the female lays from 20 to as many as 60 eggs and then covers them carefully with more debris. The eggs are incubated by the heat of the sun and also, possibly, by the heat generated by the decaying plants. Unlike most reptiles, the female alligator does not leave the nest. She stays nearby, often lying watchfully on top of the mound. Many kinds of marauders feast on alligator eggs whenever they have the chance. But the female defends the nest ferociously, even when men attack her.

When the female alligator hears her young struggling to break out of their eggs, she begins to dig away the top of the nest to help

The alligator does not incubate her eggs but keeps watch over the nest to protect it from intruders.

the little ones get out. Until the following spring the young stay close to their mother. Even so, only a few of them manage to survive, for they are preyed upon by bears, raccoons, hawks, and many other animals.

Sea turtles make spectacular journeys when they return to land to lay their eggs. Perfectly adapted to life in the water, a female turtle has great difficulty moving on land. Yet she crawls laboriously over a sandy beach to a place beyond the high-tide mark, for salt water will destroy her eggs. There she digs a deep hole in the sand. Sometimes she makes several trips from the sea to the beach before finding a spot that suits her. The digging may require several hours, for the female often digs a basin two feet deep and as much as ten feet around. In the bottom of this hole she lays a hundred or more eggs, then carefully smooths the sand again and crawls back out to sea.

Often prying human eyes watch this entire process, but the turtle seems to be so intent on accomplishing her task that she does not notice. In most places, gathering turtle

Sea turtles crawl ashore to lay their eggs in the sand above the high tide mark.

eggs for food is now prohibited by law, for turtle eggs are a great delicacy and are widely sought after.

Raccoons, bears, and other creatures that prowl the beaches delight in the discovery of a turtle's nest, too. They can feast on the eggs.

Even when the young turtles hatch and squirm their way out of the sandy nest they are in great danger. Fortunately, the hatching most often occurs at night. So the young put out to sea under cover of darkness and escape being seen by gulls, eagles, and other predators as they cross the beach to the water. At sea, they are nevertheless quite helpless for several days, for they still contain a large amount of yolk from the egg and are so buoyed up by it that they can submerge only briefly. This makes them easy prey for gulls, ospreys, and large fish.

Fresh-water turtles dig nests along shore and cover them again so carefully that they are hard to find. Tortoises, snakes, and lizards may deposit their eggs in natural crevices, burrows, or depressions in the ground. Some take more precautions than others. One of the monitor lizards of Africa hides its eggs in a termite nest.

Other reptiles have solved the problem by not laying eggs at all. They carry their eggs inside their bodies until they are ready to hatch. Some of these eggs receive food and oxygen from the blood of the mother.

When the young emerge into the world, they are born alive. Common garter snakes may bear as many as 70 young at a time. Horned toads, too, bear their young alive, as do sea snakes, most fresh-water snakes, and rattlesnakes.

A female python coils itself around its eggs to incubate them.

The Indian mongoose is famous for its readiness to attack cobras.

Enemies

REPTILES have many enemies in the animal world.

India's famous mongoose, a small agile mammal, is a killer of cobras. Skillfully it dodges the snake's strikes until finally the snake is tired out. Then it moves in swiftly and sinks its teeth into the cobra's brain.

Big pythons are eaten by leopards. Eagles and hawks prey on lizards, snakes, and turtles as frequently as they can catch them. There are lizards that regularly eat other lizards or snakes, and there are many snakes that eat lizards. Young reptiles, in particular, are preyed upon by many kinds of animals. Even bullfrogs will feast on young snakes or turtles.

In addition, reptiles are plagued by a variety of smaller organisms. Skin diseases cause blisters over their bodies or sores around their mouths. Fungus growths occur on their scales. They are also attacked by numerous parasites. Leeches cluster on turtles. Mites take up lodging under the scales of snakes and lizards. People who keep reptiles as pets are soon aware that reptiles are beset by their share of pests and ailments.

But of all the enemies of reptiles, man is the most persistent and most damaging. Since time immemorial, reptiles—especially snakes—have been misunderstood, hence persecuted. They are the subject of tales and superstitions, and their presence is rarely tolerated by men.

Great numbers are killed on highways. Turtles move too slowly to escape fast-moving automobiles. Snakes prowl the highways to feed on animals that live at the roadside, or they go there at night to get warm on the pavement.

Some reptiles have been killed in such large numbers, because of their commercial value, that they are now threatened with extinction. Hides of alligators, crocodiles, and some snakes and lizards are used to make leather. Hawksbill turtles were once hunted as a source of "tortoise shell."

Big sea turtles have long been harvested for soups and steaks. Of these, the green turtles are the most delicately flavored. In the southern Caribbean waters, where green turtles are found abundantly, their diet consists almost entirely of a green marine plant called turtle grass which grows profusely in the shallow underwater pastures. Even the fat of these turtles becomes bluish green in color. The meat of these plant eaters tastes much like veal, but if green turtles are caught snake is tired out. Then it moves in swiftly and sinks its teeth into the cobra's brain.

Big pythons are eaten by leopards. Eagles and hawks prey on lizards, snakes, and turtles as frequently as they can catch them. There are lizards that regularly eat other lizards or snakes, and there are many snakes that eat lizards. Young reptiles, in particular, are preyed upon by many kinds of animals. Even bullfrogs will feast on young snakes or turtles.

In addition, reptiles are plagued by a variety of smaller organisms. Skin diseases cause blisters over their bodies or sores around their mouths. Fungus growths occur on their scales. They are also attacked by numerous parasites. Leeches cluster on turtles. Mites take up lodging under the scales of snakes and lizards. People who keep reptiles as pets are soon aware that reptiles are beset by their share of pests and ailments.

But of all the enemies of reptiles, man is the most persistent and most damaging. Since time immemorial, reptiles—especially snakes —have been misunderstood, hence persecuted. They are the subject of tales and superstitions, and their presence is rarely tolerated by men.

Great numbers are killed on highways. Turtles move too slowly to escape fast-moving automobiles. Snakes prowl the highways to feed on animals that live at the roadside, or they go there at night to get warm on the pavement.

Some reptiles have been killed in such large numbers, because of their commercial value, that they are now threatened with extinction. Hides of alligators, crocodiles, and some snakes and lizards are used to make leather. Hawksbill turtles were once hunted as a source of "tortoise shell."

Big sea turtles have long been harvested for soups and steaks. Of these, the green turtles are the most delicately flavored. In the southern Caribbean waters, where green turtles are found abundantly, their diet consists almost entirely of a green marine plant called turtle grass which grows profusely in the shallow underwater pastures. Even the fat of these turtles becomes bluish green in color. The meat of these plant eaters tastes much like veal, but if green turtles are caught

Chicken turtles are prized as food
in southern coastal regions.

from areas where they have had to subsist on fish or shellfish, then their flesh is "fishy" in flavor.

Many fresh-water turtles are also good to eat. Snapping turtles are sold commercially in large numbers. Pound-sized diamondback terrapins once brought as much as ten dollars apiece in some restaurants. Soft-shelled turtles, gopher tortoises, and chicken turtles are among the many kinds of turtles prized throughout the world both for their meat and for their eggs.

Canned rattlesnake meat is a popular novelty food, and alligator-tail steaks were featured in Florida restaurants in days gone by when the reptiles were more common. Large lizards, however, are regular food fare in many countries. Monitors, chuckwallas, and iguanids are among those most frequently eaten. Their eggs, too, are relished.

There is no way to determine how much damage is done to the total population of these reptiles by constant and heavy slaughter. A census of reptiles is not easily made.

Many kinds of reptiles are used as food.

Iguana

Monitor

Chuckwalla

Yet careful studies do sometimes reveal strange and unsuspected roles played by reptiles in the overall scheme of life. Alligators were once slaughtered thoughtlessly in Florida's swamps. There seemed to be no good reason why they should be preserved.

Now the killing of alligators is controlled. It has been determined that alligators help to reduce mosquito populations by keeping waterway channels and sloughs open. This not only reduces the amount of stagnant water, where mosquitoes breed most prevalently, but also opens up avenues for a variety of small fish which feed on mosquito larvae. In addition, alligator holes are often the only available water supplies for many animals during the dry season. Finding the pool of water in front of an alligator's den can be like discovering an oasis in the desert.

In South America a relationship has been discovered between alligators and infestations of farm laborers with liver flukes. The life cycle of the liver fluke involves spending one stage in a fresh-water snail. If the snails are abundant, so are the liver flukes. If alligators are plentiful, then there are fewer snails and less disease—because young alligators eat the snails.

During the days of sailing vessels, the Galapagos Islands—Galapagos comes from the Spanish word meaning "tortoise"—were a regular stop for the sole purpose of loading the ships' holds with tortoises. Rolled onto their backs and wedged together, the tortoises would stay alive for many months without demanding either food or water. They were an excellent source of fresh meat during long voyages. In emergencies they could also be tapped to get fresh water, for the tortoises themselves stored it in pockets beneath the skin of their necks and legs.

Even after the whaling ships stopped visiting the islands the slaughter of the great tortoises continued, as they were then killed for their fat which was rendered into oil. And dogs and cats left on the islands turned wild and ate the eggs and the young tortoises.

No one knows how many tortoises were destroyed on the Galapagos Islands, but some estimates place the figure well into the millions. Finally, laws were passed to prevent their extinction.

The black mamba of Africa is reported to attack without provocation. This hoodless and deadly snake is a member of the cobra family.

Self-protection

REPTILES seldom bite people unless they are provoked. Then they bite to protect themselves, or in a few cases, to protect their young or their eggs. As a rule, they first try to escape.

Some African "spitting" cobras can squirt their venom with accuracy up to a distance of 12 feet. Another member of the cobra family plays dead until an animal gets close, and then it uncoils quickly and inflicts its deadly bite.

Rattlesnakes live in most parts of the United States.

Western Diamondback Rattler

In India and Pakistan, from 10,000 to 20,000 people die each year from snake bites, largely by cobras and kraits. In the United States, deaths from snake bites are rare—probably not more than 10 to 20 deaths per year out of 200 million people.

Typically, of course, the bite of a poisonous reptile is used to kill or to paralyze its prey rather than as a defense mechanism. The venom contains a digestive juice which begins to break down the tissues of the animal even before it is swallowed by the snake.

In the United States, there is one poisonous lizard (the Gila monster of the desert southwest) and three types of poisonous snakes. Two of these are pit vipers, so called because of a small pit on each side of the head between the eye and nostril. These are the rattlesnakes with more than 20 species, and moccasins (copperhead and cottonmouth).

The copperhead is a poisonous snake of the eastern United States. The poisonous cottonmouth is also known as the water moccasin.

Copperhead

Cottonmouth

The coral snakes (two in the U.S.), which are relatives of the cobras, are a third type. Drop for drop, the venom of the coral snake is most potent. It affects nerves and may cause death quickly. Cobra bites sometimes take effect so quickly that the victim dies

Scarlet Snake

Common Coral Snake

Scarlet King Snake

Coral snakes are sometimes confused with the harmless scarlet snakes or the scarlet king snakes.

within minutes. The venom of the Gila monster (and also the Mexican beaded lizard, the only other poisonous lizard in the world) is a nerve poison, too. Their venom flows from glands in their lower jaw into their mouth cavity, and then moves down grooved teeth. This method of injecting the poison is slow and inefficient. The lizards may bite and chew for several minutes before any poison reaches the wound.

The poison of the pit vipers affects the flesh and blood more than the nerves. Some of these vipers like the diamondback rattlers are extremely dangerous, while others like the copperhead and massasauga seldom, if ever, kill a healthy person.

Many snakes have mildly poisonous digestive juices which help to subdue their prey. One such group is the rear-fanged snakes. They have grooved teeth at the rear of their mouths rather than hypodermic-like fangs at the front of their mouths. Their venom, as a rule, has only a mild effect on man but may be very toxic to their prey.

Reptiles not equipped with poisons, by far the majority, protect themselves in other

The snapping turtle has no teeth but its powerful jaws can inflict severe wounds.

ways. Snapping turtles, if tantalized, will strike with the speed of a snake. Their sharp jaws can inflict deep cuts. Large snappers can sever a man's finger. Some of the monstrous sea turtles, too, can be dangerous when trapped or annoyed. Leatherbacks, the largest of the sea turtles, have been known to crunch through wooden oars as though they were made of paper. Ridley's turtle, the smallest of the sea turtles, becomes so enraged when caught that it bites furiously at anything that moves and may even die in a temper tantrum.

Many nonpoisonous snakes and lizards will bite when tormented. When these snakes strike and pull back, their hooklike teeth often tear the skin and cause profuse bleeding. But few snakes have large enough teeth to make deep wounds.

Like turtles, lizards generally only pinch hard. Occasionally they may break the skin. The damage they can do, of course, depends on their size. A big monitor lizard five or six feet long can be as formidable as an alligator or a crocodile of equal size.

The heavy, lashing tail of an enraged alligator can cause as much damage as the alligator's sharp teeth.

Anole (male)

Anole (female)

The skin of the anole changes color with its background and also with its mood.

Alligators and crocodiles have jaws studded with teeth. When they grab hold with them, they twist and roll their bodies. As dangerous as their teeth are their powerful tails, which can be lashed with great enough force to break a man's leg with one blow.

Chameleons can change their color to match their background. Anoles, or American chameleons, change their color not only according to their background but also according to their mood. An excited lizard is green; when calm, it is dusky brown. Other reptiles are variously mottled and blotched so that they are difficult to see in their natural surroundings. Often their shape helps to conceal them, too. Some have a leaf-like irregularity, and others may resemble the stiff angular branches and twigs of a tree.

The tail of the glass snake lizard may break off from its body if grasped suddenly.

Glass Lizard

Many lizards, such as common skinks and glass snakes, lose their tails when they are grabbed. The lizards hurry on their way and leave the still-wiggling tails behind them. Later the lizards grow new tails. The tail of an African skink is covered with sharp spines, and when the lizard burrows into the sand to escape being caught, it goes in head first, leaving its spiny tail to block the entrance. Another and equally spiny skink holds its tail in its mouth and rolls into a ball. The sharp spines make the lizard as hard to approach as a long-quilled porcupine.

Chuckwallas crawl into rocky crevices and then inflate their bodies so that they are wedged in tightly. Indians who hunt chuckwallas for food use sharp-pointed sticks to pierce their lungs and deflate them. An African tortoise has an extremely flexible shell, making it almost shapeless as compared to other turtles. Like the chuckwalla, it hides in rocks and inflates its lungs so that it is lodged in place.

Often, brilliant warning colors are displayed suddenly when a snake or a lizard swells its throat or lifts a frilly or horny col-

The frilled lizard will suddenly unfold a brilliant neck ruff to frighten its enemies away.

lar to frighten away an intruder. Cobras spread their "hoods" when agitated. They do this by lifting elongated ribs in their neck region and pulling the skin tightly over them. Then they weave their heads and the raised foreparts of their bodies in a threatening manner. Other snakes have brightly colored undersurfaces on their tails, which they lift and weave just as the cobras do their heads. The venomous coral snake, which is brilliantly colored with bands of black and yellow, is copied by a harmless king snake.

Most reptiles hiss by expelling the air from their lungs. Some can make their hissing sound extremely menacing. Often it is accompanied by bluffing strikes. The frilled lizard, for example, hisses and opens its mouth wide. The inside of its mouth is yellow and its teeth are large. Horned toads puff their bodies, hiss, and boldly attack their foe. Sometimes drops of blood squirt from the corners of their eyes. Many snakes vibrate their tails when they are excited. Rattle-

The hognosed snake will make a pretense of striking, and if that fails, will feign death as a method of escaping from its enemies.

snakes, of course, have built-in buzzers. They do not always rattle before they strike, however.

Some reptiles feign death to discourage attackers.

The common hognosed snake of North and Central America will put on a double-feature program for anyone willing to see it through. First the snake lifts its head and flattens its body, hissing and weaving like a cobra. It also makes false strikes, never actually opening its mouth to bite. If this fails to send its intruder scurrying, the snake then goes into Act II. This time it plays dead. It begins by writhing on the ground as though it were dying a violent death. Its tongue lolls out of its mouth in the best melodramatic manner, and it may also disgorge its last meal.

But it seems to know that a dead snake must lie on its back. Even after it has become motionless and appears to be dead, it will roll quickly onto its back if an inquisitive person tries to turn it onto its stomach. If it is a good actor, this drama succeeds in keeping it alive.

INDEX

Age of reptiles, 14–17
Alligator, 13, 17, 21, 28–29, 39–40, 50–51, 55–56, 65, 74
Alligator hole, 65
Alligator snapper, 11, 43–44
Anaconda, 11
Anole, 74–75

Basilisk, 36–37
Boa, 38–39
Box turtle, 15, 21–22, 41–42
Bushmaster, 12

Carapace, 21
Chameleon, 31, 49–50, 74–75
Chuckwalla, 76
Cobra, 16, 67–68, 70–71, 77
Copperhead, 69
Coral snake, 70
Corn snake, 47
Cottonmouth, 69
Crocodile, 13, 17, 21, 28, 39–40, 50–51, 74

Egg tooth, 53
Enemies, 60–66

Flying dragon, 36
Food, 41–51
Fringe-toed lizard, 30
Frilled lizard, 78

Galapagos tortoise, 11, 17, 66
Gavial, 13, 50
Gecko, 36, 53
Gila monster, 20–21, 69
Glass snake, 75
Green turtle, 10–11, 16–17, 27–28
Ground uta, 49

Habitation, 24–32
Hawksbill turtle, 23
Hibernation, 8
Hognosed snake, 79

Iguana, 13, 28, 50

Komodo dragon, 12–13, 50

Leatherback turtle, 10, 72
Long-nosed tree snake, 32
Loggerhead turtle, 34

Mamba, 67

Nests, 53, 58

Plastron, 21
Pit vipers, 69, 71
Poisonous reptiles, 67–71
Python, 11, 38–39, 53–54

Rattlesnakes, 69

Sea snakes, 26–27
Sea turtles, 10, 27, 56–58
Scales, 5, 18–21
Shells, 21–23
Scarlet snake, 70
Skins, 5, 18–20
Skinks, 54–55
Snapping turtle, 72
Speed, 33–40
Species, 9

Temperature, 6–8
Tortoises, 11, 14, 17, 56–59, 66
Tuatara, 8

Whipsnakes, 40

BCDEFGH